ONE DAY AT A TIME

ONE DAY AT A TIME

Hope and inspiration for your chronic illness journey

By Robin Dix

Copyright © 2017 Robin Dix

All rights reserved. No part of this publication may be reproduced, distributed, or transmitted in any form or by any means, including photocopying, recording, or other electronic or mechanical methods, without the prior written permission of the publisher, except in the case of brief quotations embodied in reviews and certain other non-commercial uses permitted by copyright law.

Edited by Theresa Wegand

Cover Design by fiverr.com

ISBN-10: 1976071224

ISBN-13: 978-1976071225

Dedication

I would like to dedicate this book to all the incredible women in my Facebook group, "In Spite of My Illness." These precious women have added so much to my life, and I'm grateful to each and every one of them.

Acknowledgments

I would like to acknowledge my husband David, who is my biggest cheerleader and encouraged me every step of the way. He believed in me when I wasn't sure I believed in myself. His love is more precious than gold.

Table of Contents

Introduction 1
1: Pain is a Gift 3
2: Prayer Changes Things 5
3: Don't Lose Hope 7
4: Respect Your Limitations 9
5: Grieve the Loss of Who You Were 11
6: Embrace Your New Normal 13
7: Lean into Your Gifting 15
8: We Live in a Broken World 17
9: Release Through Worship 19
10: Self-Love 21
11: It's Ok to Say No 23
12: Asking for Help Shows Strength 25
13: Can Illness Be a Blessing? 27
14: No Guilt Parent 29
15: God Has a Plan 31
16: To Church or Not to Church 33
17: Keep Your Friends Close 35
18: Social Isolation 37
19: Blessed to Be a Blessing 39
20: Healing Hope 41
21: Educate Others 43
22: Ministry to The Broken 45
23: Heavenly Solace 47

24: Online Community 49
25: Joy in the Journey 51
26: He Will Give You Rest 53
27: Faith Not Fear 55
28: Balm of The Psalms 57
29: Breath Prayers 59
30: Compassion and Empathy 61
31: Your Life is a Tapestry 63
Resources 65
About the Author 67

INTRODUCTION

As a Christian, I've found very few devotionals written for those of us battling chronic illness. Sometimes it's just hard to keep our faith intact. We need to be assured that God is with us every step of the way. I have written this devotional to help you connect your faith to your illness. I never want you to feel alone on this unpredictable journey.

You are precious in His sight, and He is holding you in the palm of His hand. My purpose in writing is to take some of the issues we face and allow God to minister to you in the midst.

I've had multiple chronic illnesses for many years, and I've been blessed to meet and support over 800 women who also struggle with chronic illness. I'm trusting that this devotional will speak to your heart, bring you hope, and will be a word in season for your soul. God has used me over the years to touch many lives, and for that, I'm truly grateful and blessed.

I will send you a copy of my *10 Commandments for Chronic Illness* as a thank you for purchasing this book; just send an email to: robindixwrites@gmail.com. As you read, I pray that your faith will grow and that you will be able to surrender your illness to the only One who has your best interests in mind.

The table of contents will help you decide which devotion is drawing you on a given day. Feel free to jump around. I would love to hear from you after you've had the opportunity to read this book!

1: PAIN IS A GIFT

"Dear brothers and sisters, when troubles come your way, consider it an opportunity for great joy."
(James 1:2 NLT)

I see pain as a gift. It refines us, rearranges our priorities, and draws us closer to the Father. Chronic illness brings its own kind of pain, both physical and emotional. It took time for me to see pain as a gift, and if you're new to this chronic illness journey, it may take some time for you to get there too. That's ok.

Pain doesn't come gift wrapped in beautiful paper with a lovely bow attached. It's disruptive, time-consuming, unwanted, and undesired. But God uses our pain to minister to others, and that's a gift.

Pain allows others to bring help and hope to us, and that's a gift.

Pain whittles away the dross in our life, leaving only what's truly important, and that's a gift.

Pain causes our hearts to cry out to God, and that's a gift.

Pain is no respecter of persons, and it draws us together, and that's a gift.

Pain causes us to become part of a different community, making friends we otherwise would not have had, and that's a gift.

Let's embrace this paradigm shift and see our pain as a gift from the hand of the One who loves us more than we could ever fully comprehend. Allow Him to take your pain and create out of it a thing of beauty that showcases His amazing grace.

Father God, I surrender my pain to You and ask that You would make it something that will keep me close to You. Help me to see it as a gift that You have entrusted to me. I praise You even in my pain. Amen.

2: PRAYER CHANGES THINGS

"Don't worry about anything; instead, pray about everything. Tell God what you need, and thank him for all he has done. Then you will experience God's peace, which exceeds anything we can understand. His peace will guard your hearts and minds as you live in Christ Jesus." (Philippians 4:6,7 NLT)

Prayer changes things, but mostly it changes us. I love that God's word tells us to pray about *everything*. That means that there is nothing too small that He couldn't be bothered with and nothing so big that He can't handle it. Your illness matters to God.

You have the privilege of praying for others, and in so doing, you will be blessed. If someone offers to pray for you, allow them to. Be honest about what you want prayer for, and let them know you're open to whatever God has planned for you, no expectations. Don't rob them of this blessing.

Ask God to reveal to you His purpose for this season in your life. If you're unable to work a 9-5 job, this is the perfect time to polish off those dreams and see how you can make money from home, doing something you love. Ask others to pray for you as well that God would open some unexpected doors for you. God has provided opportunities for me to write, and I'm so grateful for that.

Sometimes our prayers are passionate and full of worship. At other times, it's just Help! God understands your struggles and your pain; His Son suffered too. He is well acquainted with pain and grief, loss and tears. Let Him comfort you today.

ROBIN DIX

Father God, what a privilege you have given me to come to you with everything that's on my heart: praise and pity, joy and incredible pain. Help me to know that prayer is as important as the air I breathe. I praise you even in my suffering. Amen.

3: DON'T LOSE HOPE

"Let us hold tightly without wavering to the hope we affirm, for God can be trusted to keep his promise." (Hebrews 10:23 NLT)

Hope is what gets us through the bad days. It's what keeps us holding on when we just want to give up. Hope is not just your state of mind; it's your state of heart. It's more than just pulling yourself up by the bootstraps; it's trusting the heart of your Father and knowing He will *never* let you down or let you go.

If we lose hope, it will feel as though there is nothing left to live for. That's a lie from the pit of hell. Even on our darkest days, we need to hold onto hope for all we're worth. Hope deferred does indeed make our heart sick.

Never give up hope that one day you will be healed. It may not happen in this life, but as a believer, it will definitely happen when God calls you home. Hope looks forward to the future. It's life giving and dynamic.

"Hope always has a future. It leans forward with expectation. It desires to plan for tomorrow. And that opens us up to greater possibilities. Are you looking forward? Do you have hope for the future? If you have high expectations for tomorrow, then you probably want to meet it at your best. How do you do that? By growing, learning, and improving. Lack of hope breeds indifference toward the future. Hope brings motivation." (Maxwell, John. "Hope, the Motivation of Learning." The John Maxwell Co. http://www.johnmaxwell.com/blog/hope-the-motivation-of-learning)

Hold onto hope.

Father God, please infuse me with Your supernatural hope. I desperately need a fresh infusion that only You can bring. Help me never to lose my hope. You are more than able, and I am more than willing to receive it daily. Amen.

4: RESPECT YOUR LIMITATIONS

"So let us come boldly to the throne of our gracious God. There we will receive his mercy, and we will find grace to help us when we need it most."
(Hebrews 4:16 NLT)

I think one of the hardest things to acknowledge is that we have limitations. We all as a human race have limitations, but those of us with chronic illness have them glaringly obvious, to ourselves anyway.

But I believe that God will use your physical and emotional limitations to refine you. They will help you to grow, mature, and become more like Jesus. But only if you choose to allow it.

Some of the ways you should respect your limitations are by not overdoing things, over extending yourself, and neglecting good self-care. When you're not aware of your limitations, you can run into physical exhaustion and potentially cause yourself a flare-up. That's not good for anyone.

Pay attention to the cues that your body sends you. An important piece of that is learning to say no to invitations, big shopping trips, working overtime, and taking your kids everywhere.

On your good days, you may tend to overdo because you feel pretty good, but that can put you in bed for days afterward. Trust God for the grace and wisdom to take your illness one day, one step, at a time.

Father God, help me to respect the limitations that have been imposed on me for now. Help me to never give up on the possibility of a cure or supernatural healing. I surrender these limitations to you and praise your holy name! Amen.

5: GRIEVE THE LOSS OF WHO YOU WERE

**"I will never forget this awful time, as I grieve over my loss."
(Lamentations 3:20 NLT)**

God has given you the gift of grief. It is a precious time where you can express sorrow over the things and people you have lost. When you became chronically ill, you experienced the devastating loss of who you once were. Allow yourself to grieve that loss.

Sadness, depression, crying, anger, and acceptance are all a part of this journey of grief. Grief has no timetable and no protocol. Everyone grieves differently and for different lengths of time. Just when you think you're past it, something may happen that pulls you back in. Give it time.

It's *normal* to grieve the loss of who you used to be and weep over the things you were once capable of doing. Pain and fatigue have a way of leveling the playing field. Allow yourself to grieve. Don't stuff your feelings.

The Holy Spirit is your comforter; let Him comfort you during this tumultuous time. He's a gentleman and waits to be asked. Just ask. It's that simple, but not necessarily that easy. Your anger may prevent you from reaching out at times, but God understands. Don't beat yourself up or feel guilty for that.

Eventually you *will* come to a place of peace and acceptance. It doesn't mean that you're happy about it, but you trust your Father's plan for you. You will then be able to search for ways to minister to others and look for new ways to live your life with joy.

ROBIN DIX

Father God, thank you for the gift of grief. Help me to get through this process and become better and not bitter. Holy Spirit wrap your comforting arms around me as I work through my grief. I desire to honor you even in this, Lord. Amen.

6: EMBRACE YOUR NEW NORMAL

"He will take our weak mortal bodies and change them into glorious bodies like his own, using the same power with which he will bring everything under his control." (Philippians 3:21 NLT)

I find it interesting that, when things were going well and I was healthy, I thought it would always be that way. But God chose a different path for you and me, and though I don't understand why, I do believe that He would have us embrace our new normal.

I'm still in the process of accepting my new normal after many years of being sick. I think that, like most things in life, it goes in cycles. Perhaps you're wondering what they even look like.

Sleeping all the time? New normal.

Using a cane, walker, or wheelchair? New normal.

Only able to walk for five minutes? New normal.

Need a pill organizer for all those meds? New normal.

No longer able to drive? New normal.

Need help to cook and clean? New normal.

You get the picture. It's a waste of emotional resources to wish things were back the way they were. Be present in today and keep moving forward into your tomorrows. Change is hard, right? We are comfortable with the status quo. We don't want our boat rocked.

As a believer, you need to lean hard on Jesus and make scripture your compass, not your illness. Remember that He says He will *never* leave you when you feel lonely. Even though your health and circumstances change, He is *always* the same.

Father God, help me not to fight against my new normal, but to trust Your heart toward me. Someday my new normal will be a new body, and I really look forward to that day!! Thank you, precious Lord. Amen.

7: LEAN INTO YOUR GIFTING

"God has given each of you a gift from his great variety of spiritual gifts. Use them well to serve one another."
(1 Peter 4:10 NLT)

Each of us has a gift, even though we thought God wouldn't continue to use us in our broken state. Perhaps you are ill for such a time as this. God has you in the palm of His hand and wants you to use your spiritual gifts to honor Him and bless others.

At the moment of salvation, as a believer, you receive one of seven motivational gifts. They include prophecy, serving, teaching, exhorting, giving, organizing, or mercy. A motivational gift can be compared to a pair of eyeglasses sent from God, given so that you can see people and circumstances through that particular set of "lenses."

You have a unique set of gifts from God, given specifically for you to use in the church and in your own personal life. Being chronically ill doesn't change that. It may change the way you use your gifts. Trust God to show you how to use your gifts.

For example, one of my gifts is the gift of mercy. God is showing me ways to use that gift in this new season of my life. I have a Facebook group for chronically ill women, where I make myself available when people need a listening ear and a compassionate heart. I'm blessed and humbled to use the gifts God has blessed me with.

ROBIN DIX

Father God, I praise You and thank You for giving me a unique set of gifts. Help me to use them to bring honor to You and be a blessing to others. Show me what my gifts are. May You always be glorified in all that I do! Amen.

8: WE LIVE IN A BROKEN WORLD

"For the Lord protects the bones of the righteous; not one of them is broken!" (Psalm 34:20 NLT)

Oftentimes we wonder why we even have sickness. Is it because of something we did or didn't do? No, it's because we live in a fallen and broken world. Broken by sin.

I know you would not set out to choose to have a chronic illness, and neither would I. But God has chosen you and me to endure this. It's only for a brief moment of time compared to all eternity. But I know it can feel *long*.

Sickness *is* a result of sin, but not yours or mine. It's the sin of Adam and Eve, which broke the world . . . for a time. Even Paul had a thorn in the flesh that very well could have been an illness. Even though he longed to stay here and serve Christ, he yearned all the more for his heavenly home.

Often, we ask ourselves, "Why me?" The better questions to ask would be, "Why not me?" and "What now, Lord?" I want God to use me in any way He chooses in this season of my life. But there are days . . .

Don't let people tell you that, if you had enough faith, you would be healed, or if there wasn't sin in your life, you wouldn't be sick. Those are lies of the enemy, and he'd like nothing more than to have you blame yourself. We know where the real blame lies.

ROBIN DIX

Father God, I thank You that, even though I live in a fallen and broken world right now, you are preparing a place for me in heaven. Help me to persevere while I am here and close my ears to the lies of the enemy. I praise You Lord every day! Amen.

9: RELEASE THROUGH WORSHIP

"But the time is coming—indeed it's here now—when true worshipers will worship the Father in spirit and in truth. The Father is looking for those who will worship him that way." (John 4:23 NLT)

I find that the best way to release frustrations and fear is through worship. I find a worship song that fits my situation or just speaks to my heart, and I close my eyes and lose myself in worship to the King.

When you worship, your praise releases the power of God in your life. It also sends the enemy of your soul running because he cannot be in the presence of a holy God.

Worship is more than just singing and lifting of your hands. It's a lifestyle, a mindset. You can stop any minute of the day and lift your voice in praise and thanksgiving as you pray. God truly does inhabit the praises of His people!

When you worship God, you release His supernatural power into your situation. When you surrender your pain and other symptoms and lay them at the foot of the cross, you acknowledge that Jesus died for your sickness and pain, and you choose to lift up His name and praise Him in the midst of all you are suffering.

Worship enables the breaking of curses and chains that have held you captive. It releases the power of the Holy Spirit to move in your life and bring the comfort only He can. Lift your hands today and begin to worship the God who created you and longs to show His incredible love to you.

ROBIN DIX

Father God, free me to worship You and praise Your holy name! I desire to give You all the glory as I surrender to Your plan for my life. You alone are worthy of all honor and praise and worship! Amen.

10: SELF-LOVE

"No one hates his own body but feeds and cares for it . . ." (Ephesians 5:29 NLT)

Loving yourself means taking time for yourself and engaging in self-caring activities. Pain, fatigue, family life, appointments, etc. take so much from you. You will feel depleted if you don't make a conscious effort to make the time for self-care.

If you are to love your neighbor as yourself, as scripture admonishes you in Mark 12:31, well that necessitates that you love yourself, right? Maybe you think this is selfish, but it's so important to your sense of well-being. Self-Love is not selfish; it is self-caring.

Why not take a bubble bath, a walk to enjoy nature, read an engaging book, sit on the beach, blow bubbles, draw or paint, make a gratitude journal? There are any number of ways you can love yourself.

Self-expression is another important piece. If you always say negative things to yourself, it will affect your health. Don't allow yourself to say things like, "I don't feel good," "I'm never going to feel better," "God doesn't care about me," or "I must deserve this." Those are lies straight from the pit of hell.

Instead, say things like, "I'm worthy," "I'm getting better," "God is for me," or "I am blessed." You get the picture. You can even write them on sticky notes and put them where you'll see them. Write them on your heart, your mirror, your wall, your doorposts. Let go of that stinkin' thinkin'.

ROBIN DIX

Father God, you loved me enough to send Jesus to die for me. I really can't even begin to grasp the depth of your love for me, but I know it's amazing! Help me to love myself as you love me, and do what I can to love those around me as well. I love you Lord! Amen.

11: IT'S OK TO SAY NO

"Just say a simple, 'Yes, I will,' or 'No, I won't.' Anything beyond this is from the evil one."
(Matthew 5:37 NLT)

When you struggle with saying "no," let me reassure you that it's ok to say "no." Before you got sick, you probably wouldn't have had cause to say "no" too often because your ability to do things and go places was not an issue.

Now that you have greater limitations and bad days, you need to learn to say "no." You should say "yes" as often as you're able. Therein lies the rub, doesn't it? You really want to say "yes" to things you know you need to say "no" to.

Some things you should say "yes" to because they're important, even though you know you will pay for it later, such as your child's graduation, your son or daughter's wedding, or a funeral of a loved one.

It's ok to say "no" to a family gathering, a party, coffee with a friend, an appointment, a baby shower, etc.

You should say "yes" as often as you know you are able and it won't compromise your health. If you're experiencing a flare-up, you should care enough about yourself to say "no." I learned as a parent to say "yes" to my children as often as I could so that, when I had to say "no," they knew I really couldn't say "yes."

ROBIN DIX

Father God, touch me please and let me know deep in my heart that it's ok to say no when I need to. Help me to be aware of when those times are. Give me wisdom and discernment daily as I walk this chronic illness journey. Amen.

12: ASKING FOR HELP SHOWS STRENGTH

"Keep on asking, and you will receive what you ask for. Keep on seeking, and you will find. Keep on knocking, and the door will be opened to you."
(Matthew 7:7 NLT)

I know that our society tends to make you feel that asking for help is a sign of weakness, but it actually shows strength: strength of character, strength in the face of illness, strength in being willing to set aside your pride.

It's not usually easy to ask for help, especially when you feel so needy all the time. Am I right? There may also be people in your life that make it very difficult for you to ask them for any kind of help. Ask anyway.

Trust the Lord to provide all the help you need daily, being willing to accept that it might not come in the way you expect. Don't be afraid to make use of community sources of help as well. There are community centers in many places that depend on volunteers, and they can provide rides to medical appointments or take you grocery shopping.

Jesus calls you to be strong and courageous, but He never said it would be easy. Keep a list of people and resources you can call on when you need them. Don't trust that foggy thinking; you know how undependable that is. If you have a smartphone, you can keep your list in your notes app.

ROBIN DIX

Father God, help me to know that asking for help, whether from you or others, comes from a place of strength and not of weakness. When I deny others the privilege of helping, I am robbing them of a blessing as well. I know my help ultimately comes from your hand as you move in the hearts of others, and I'm so thankful! Amen.

13: CAN ILLNESS BE A BLESSING?

"That is why we never give up. Though our bodies are dying, our spirits are being renewed every day. For our present troubles are small and won't last very long. Yet they produce for us a glory that vastly outweighs them and will last forever!" (2 Corinthians 4:16,17 NLT)

There are a lot of true believers who feel that if you just had enough faith you would be healed. I have a problem with that because I know some very godly people with a lot of faith who have not been healed. I don't see anywhere in scripture where it says we will all be healed in this lifetime. However, we absolutely will be in the next.

So, can your chronic illness be a blessing? I believe it can. As you reach out to others who are also suffering, you will be blessed. As you lean more on your Heavenly Father and less on your own strength, I believe you will be blessed.

God has a plan and a purpose for your life and mine, and the enemy of our soul does all he can to thwart that. Does that mean you should just sit back and stop praying for healing? Absolutely not! God can heal us, and He will when the time is right.

Don't let others cause you to believe that it's your fault that you are not well. While there may very well be issues in your life that have triggered your illness, that is not how God treats those He calls His own. Keep praying and believing, but keep being a blessing to others and allow others to bless you.

Father God, I don't know why you have not chosen to heal me yet, but I absolutely believe that You can. Help my life to be a blessing to others, and help me to close my ears to those who would heap unholy guilt on me for my illness. I love you so much! Amen.

14: NO GUILT PARENT

"Declare me not guilty, O Lord my God, for you give justice. Don't let my enemies laugh about me in my troubles." (Psalm 35:24 NLT)

When you are a parent, especially of young children, it's hard not to feel guilty. It's super important to take care of *yourself* so that you can better care for your children. Don't feel guilty or even selfish because this is the right thing to do.

What kinds of things might bring in that parent guilt? Missing a sporting event or school event. Not having the energy to throw a birthday party or even go to the park. Not being able to drive their friends to the mall or go see a movie. Not having the energy to bake for the bake sale or chaperone a field trip.

As they get older, different issues arise. Not being able to take them driving or to wait while they take their road test. Having to leave early from their graduation or wedding reception. Being unable to babysit your grandchildren for the weekend or do lots of fun things with them.

Yes, your illness prevents you from some things, but you should never feel regret. Do the things you can and teach your children to be compassionate, not only towards you, but also to others who have limitations, visible and not so visible. Read to them, pray with and for them. Sing silly songs together. Have fun in the ways that you're able.

Father God, help me to recognize that guilt comes from the enemy when it comes to us parents. Enable me to be the best parent I can be as I desire to walk in Your mercy and grace. I surrender my parenting and limitations to You and lay them at Your feet. Amen.

15: GOD HAS A PLAN

"'For I know the plans I have for you,' says the Lord. 'They are plans for good and not for disaster, to give you a future and a hope.'" (Jeremiah 29:11 NLT)

I know it's hard to imagine that God has a plan for good in your life when you're struggling with your chronic illness. He does. He wants to give you a future and a hope. Precious gifts indeed.

You may have recently been diagnosed or you may have been ill for years. Either way, God has a plan for you in this season of your life. Ask Him to show you what it is He wants you to be doing.

Whom can you encourage? Whom can you serve? Whom can you send a card to or make a much-appreciated phone call to?

God sees your loneliness, and He desires to comfort you. He understands your limitations and wants to meet all your needs. He sees your heart that desires to honor Him, and He wants to bless that.

Daily ask God to continue to unfold His plan for you; then watch for ways He's doing just that. His heart is for you, always! Trust His plan, surrender your own, and enjoy the journey set before you.

Father God, especially on days when I am in a flare, it's so hard to see clearly that You do have a plan to give me a future and a hope. I know that this illness is the result of living in a broken and fallen world. I just want to praise You that your ultimate plan is my healing, whether now or in the next life. I trust You. Amen.

ROBIN DIX

16: TO CHURCH OR NOT TO CHURCH

"Please give my greetings to our brothers and sisters at Laodicea, and to Nympha and the church that meets in her house." (Colossians 4:15 NLT)

There are times when you will not be able to get out and go to "church." The church is not a building but the family of God. Personally, I love the idea of a home church. It's more personal, and you get to know one another and pray together. I once attended a home church where we had a meal together first. It really bonded us.

There are also small group Bible studies and online services you can take advantage of. Do what works best for you, and don't feel guilty about it. You are *not* being selfish, lazy, or sinful if you miss church. You are suffering and struggling with pain and fatigue. God understands.

People won't always understand why you're not there (unless they know you really well), but you don't owe anyone an explanation other than you weren't feeling well. Others may tell you that you are not being faithful, and they may even question your salvation. Be like a duck and let those kinds of comments roll off your back.

Spend time worshipping God, reading His Word, spending time in prayer, and allowing Him to minister to you. Do the best you can, and trust Him to work out the details. Perhaps you could invite a friend or neighbor to join you. Remember where two or more are gathered, He is in their midst.

Father God, you know my heart and how much I long to be with other believers. Give me a plan for those times that I am unable to be at church. I still long for fellowship and ask that You'd provide the best solution for me. I trust You Lord! Amen.

17: KEEP YOUR FRIENDS CLOSE

"My loved ones and friends stay away, fearing my disease. Even my own family stands at a distance."
(Psalm 38:11 NLT)

It's difficult when your friends seem to gradually abandon you once you become ill. Their lives may be busy, and perhaps they feel that they can't slow down enough to engage with you now that you're limited in the things you can do.

I know you would enjoy a phone call, a card in the mail, having them drop by for a cup of tea. It seems as though the brakes have been slammed on in your life, while your friends are on cruise control going a cool 65 mph. You may be asking what that has to do with keeping your friends close.

Instead of waiting for your friend to have time for you, initiate ways you can make that happen, letting your friend know that your illness may cause you to cancel at the last minute, but not to take it personally because you really do want to spend time with her.

Leave a loving message on her cell phone. Send a card saying that you miss her, and ask if next week sometime would work out to get together for coffee and catching up. Send her a book that you think she'd enjoy, enclosing a personal note. Keep the fires of friendship alive. Pray for your friend and her family, and let her know you are blessed to pray for her.

Father God, friendship is Your idea, and I ask that you help me to keep my friends close, especially when they want to pull away.

Give me wisdom to know how to reach out to them. Help me have grace for them and extend mercy and forgiveness when needed. Help me not to wallow in self-pity but continue to find ways to enjoy my friends, despite my illness. Amen.

18: SOCIAL ISOLATION

"Turn to me and have mercy, for I am alone and in deep distress."
(Psalm 25:16 NLT)

One of the worst things about chronic illness is the social isolation. Is this something you are struggling with? You are not alone. Sitting on the sidelines and watching your friends do the things you used to be able to do is very hard indeed.

You need to speak up and let your friends know you would really enjoy their company. Ask them not to stop inviting you places because, when you're able, you'd love to go. It's hard to take the initiative sometimes, because honestly, you may not be up for it.

Another thing you could do is join a Bible study or support group. There are also lots of online groups or forums you can take part in. It will really help you feel less alone and isolated. I will post some groups and websites in the resources section. Also, check on Facebook for a group that fits your needs.

It's more than just missing out on activities; it's really missing the connections you had with family and friends. We all have a God-given need to belong, to be part of a community. Fortunately, for the times when you can't get out, there are online groups on various social media platforms where you can get connected. Take advantage of those.

Father God, I ask that you bring people into my life that I can connect with and draw strength from in my times of isolation. Meet my every need through Your riches in Christ Jesus, and help me to be a blessing to others who are also working through their chronic illness. Amen.

19: BLESSED TO BE A BLESSING

"Don't repay evil for evil. Don't retaliate with insults when people insult you. Instead, pay them back with a blessing. That is what God has called you to do, and he will grant you his blessing." (1 Peter 3:9 NLT)

Did you know that when you are blessed by something someone does for you that you have also been a blessing to them? It's true. So, when someone offers to do something for you and you decline due to pride, you are robbing yourself *and* them of a blessing. Keep that in mind the next time someone offers to go shopping for you, pick up your prescriptions, take your kiddos to the park, or clean your bathroom.

I'm sure you've had plenty of opportunities to help others. Maybe you talked them through a rough patch, sent them a card letting them know you're thinking of them, made a playlist of music that you know they'd enjoy. Remember how blessed you felt to do that?

God has promised to bless us, and out of the abundance of His blessings, we should bless others. If God has blessed you with the gift of creativity, use that gift to create something like a baby blanket. If God has blessed you with the gift of gab, use that to give a word of encouragement. Ask God to show you how you can be a blessing to others, and you'll feel blessed in return as a beautiful reward for your faithfulness.

Father God, help me to bless those around me with the gifts and abilities you have given to me. Open doors I might not have otherwise noticed. Give me the desire to walk through those doors and equip me to minister to the needs of those you bring to my attention. My desire is to serve You and bring You glory! Amen.

20: HEALING HOPE

"Then you will have healing for your body and strength for your bones." (Proverbs 3:8 NLT)

You should never give up hope for healing. I absolutely believe in healing for the here and now. I also believe that, while we are waiting for our healing, God has a plan and a purpose for such a time as this.

You may have the faith required for your healing, but God may have a different plan for you. Perhaps he's developing in you a deeper compassion and a greater empathy for those who are suffering, as well as working out your salvation while you are here.

I absolutely believe that God could heal you in a heartbeat. Even if He chooses not to heal you here, you can be assured of your healing in heaven.

Trust in his plan for you. Trust that his love for you is beyond human comprehension. Trust that his plans for you are good and will give you hope and a future.

Never give up hope. Use this time to reach out to others who are also suffering with chronic illness. You understand them in a way that many people will not. Ask the Lord to show you what you could be doing during this time of waiting. Don't waste it feeling sorry for yourself.

Father God, birth in me a strong hope for the healing you have for me. Help me to trust in Your timing and not mine. Help me to give the gift of hope to others who don't yet know You. Help me not to waste this time in my life. My heart's deepest desire is to do Your will always. Amen.

21: EDUCATE OTHERS

"And the Spirit of the Lord will rest on him— the Spirit of wisdom and understanding, the Spirit of counsel and might, the Spirit of knowledge and the fear of the Lord." (Isaiah 11:2 NLT)

God allows circumstances in your life not only to teach you something but so that you can use those experiences to teach others. If you have learned things that would benefit others who are also suffering, then you have an obligation to help them.

Perhaps you have found some shortcuts to cleaning your home. Or maybe you have found some ways to alleviate pain and discomfort. If so, then you shouldn't keep that information and knowledge to yourself. Rather, use it to equip others.

I bet you could start a group on Facebook and invite some other women who are suffering and you could all learn from each other. God has entrusted you with this precious gift of suffering. Ask him how He wants you to use this to bless and encourage others.

I have great faith in you to use the knowledge you have acquired through your unique experiences, and that you would be willing to pass it on to others. Become a teacher to the broken and hurting. You can do this.

Father God, there are so many times when I feel so helpless. But you are always here for me, every day, in all my suffering. Help me to help others with the knowledge and experiences that you have allowed me to endure. I choose not to waste any of them while I have breath. Amen.

ROBIN DIX

22: MINISTRY TO THE BROKEN

"The Lord is close to the brokenhearted; he rescues those whose spirits are crushed." (Psalm 34:18 NLT)

You have been inducted into the ministry to the broken-hearted. God does not waste anything in our lives. He has chosen you to minister to those who really need it—because you understand.

I'm not saying that God purposely made you chronically ill so that you could minister to others. What I am saying is that, because you are now chronically ill, you have a ministry opportunity that others don't have.

As a believer, you have the privilege of praying for and ministering to others. He's asking you to do that today. Will you respond to the call?

I know that you are also broken and out of that brokenness you are equipped to minister to others. People are out there waiting for someone to come along beside them and just be with them. Perhaps reading the book of Job would help you to gain a different perspective.

I wish we could get together over a cup of tea and pray together. I wish we could share with each other our struggles, our good times, and the things that God is teaching us. You are so important to God and to me. Let's get this ministry started, shall we?

Father God, only You can equip me to minister to other broken people. I desire this anointing and Your hand of blessing upon me in a powerful way. Bring the people to me that You would have me minister to. I surrender my heart and my plans to You. Amen.

23: HEAVENLY SOLACE

"When doubts filled my mind, your comfort gave me renewed hope and cheer." (Psalm 94:19 NLT)

No one can comfort your heart as your Heavenly Father can. He desires to comfort you and fill you with His peace, which surpasses all human comprehension. When doubts fill your mind (and they will from time to time), allow Him to renew your hope.

It doesn't have to stop there. Use the comfort you receive from God to comfort the hurting He places in your path. Don't hibernate in your pain or hoard the comfort you've been given. Enjoy the heavenly solace rained down upon you. Soak in it.

God knows that it's hard for some of you to be hugged or touched at times because it causes physical pain and discomfort. But His comfort wraps you in His arms internally and allows His peace to flow through every cell in your body.

If you are a parent, then you know how precious it is to comfort your children when they are hurting. God's comfort is so much purer and deeper than we can even imagine as parents. Let Him hold you, just hold you.

Don't seek your solace from earthly pleasures but from the heart of the Father who has loved you so incredibly much before you were even born. Don't let the enemy distract you with temporary comfort measures such as food or shopping. Allow the Holy Spirit to comfort you and increase your capacity to receive your Father's love.

Father God, help me not to settle for temporary earthly comfort, but to always seek Your amazing heavenly solace. Thank you for sending the Holy Spirit to comfort me at all times. You are a gracious and loving Father and I worship you! Amen.

24: ONLINE COMMUNITY

"Let us think of ways to motivate one another to acts of love and good works. And let us not neglect our meeting together, as some people do, but encourage one another, especially now that the day of his return is drawing near." (Hebrews 10:24-25 NLT)

As believers, we are called to be part of a community. For those of us who are chronically ill, it's not always easy to get to church. Perhaps you've heard of or even experienced streaming church services online. Although that's not the best, it still allows you to feel part of a community.

Attending online Bible studies is another way to stay connected to the community of believers. There are online Facebook groups for most illnesses, which are geared to believers as well. I would encourage you to search for ones that speak to your heart.

Being chronically ill can be a very lonely business, especially if you are dealing with extreme fatigue. The loneliness can be overwhelming at times. Perhaps you can find a prayer partner that you can get together with, enjoy a cup of tea, and pray together.

If you are part of a local congregation, let your pastor know of your situation. See if you can receive communion at home when you're unable to attend church. Perhaps you can start or participate in a prayer chain or a ministry of setting up meals for new moms and others in need.

Father God, I believe You call us to community because that's how we thrive and grow the best. When that's not possible, please lead me to online communities that can bless me and that I can be a blessing to in return. Show me your way, Father. Amen.

25: JOY IN THE JOURNEY

"Tears of joy will stream down their faces, and I will lead them home with great care. They will walk beside quiet streams and on smooth paths where they will not stumble . . ." (Jeremiah 31:9 NLT)

I know this journey has been hard, so hard, but God wants to fill you with His joy. Joy does not depend on our circumstances or our emotional landscape. It's not the same as being happy, which is so fickle at best.

Joy is a fruit of the Holy Spirit. The Spirit gives us eyes to see the beauty of Jesus, which calls joy up out of our hearts. It's a gift to you that goes deep into your spirit and affects your ability to feel God's joy. When you can see Jesus in your circumstances, then your heart is drawn out in joy towards Him.

I love what Pastor Rick Warren says about joy: "Joy is the settled assurance that God is in control of all the details of my life, the quiet confidence that *ultimately* everything is going to be alright, and the determined choice to praise God in every situation."

In her inspiring book, *Choose Joy: Because Happiness Isn't Enough*, Kay Warren teaches women what joy really is, where to find it, and how to choose it in the good times and the bad. With compassion and wisdom, she shows readers—even those who live with the constant companions of discouragement and depression—that true joy is deeper, richer, and more accessible than they might think.

ROBIN DIX

Father God, help me to choose joy and not settle for the fickleness of happiness, which changes with my circumstances. Holy Spirit, fill my heart with the joy of the Lord and help me to rejoice in all things. I can only do this by Your grace. Amen.

26: HE WILL GIVE YOU REST

"Then Jesus said, 'Come to me, all of you who are weary and carry heavy burdens, and I will give you rest. Take my yoke upon you. Let me teach you, because I am humble and gentle at heart, and you will find rest for your souls. For my yoke is easy to bear, and the burden I give you is light.'"
(Matthew 11:28-30 NLT)

If fatigue is a part of your illness journey, I can empathize. Fatigue is a major component of three chronic illnesses I currently battle. Quite often, it keeps me in bed, which, by the way, is where I do all of my writing.

Fatigue can be so wearying, but I'm so thankful that Jesus says, "Come to me, all of you who are weary and carry heavy burdens, and I will give you rest." (Matthew 11:28 NLT) Sometimes you need physical rest, but sometimes it's mental or emotional. Aren't you glad that Your Savior knows what you need and is so ready and willing to meet those needs? You just need to come to Him.

There is a great online ministry to those believers who suffer with chronic illness. The founder of *Rest Ministries* is Lisa Copen. I encourage you to check it out; she has lots of great resources.

You are weary and carrying a heavy burden; come to Jesus and get the rest your body and soul craves. He's waiting for you with open arms. Climb up into His lap . . . and just rest.

Father God, so often I feel that I must stay busy, but You invite me to come and enter Your rest. You assure me that Your yoke is easy and Your burden is light. Slow me down. Lift my face so I can gaze into Your eyes of love and trust You more completely than I ever have. Amen.

27: FAITH NOT FEAR

"It was by faith that Moses left the land of Egypt, not fearing the king's anger. He kept right on going because he kept his eyes on the one who is invisible."
(Hebrews 11:27 NLT)

It's so easy to give into fear. Fear of how you are going to care of yourself. Fear of side effects of your medications. Fear of the loss of or criticism of your family or friends. Fear of losing your job. Fear of being alone. Fear of getting sicker.

Fear is not a sin; it's an emotional state of mind. Jesus doesn't want you to be afraid; lean on Him. Bring all your fears to Him, lay them at the foot of the cross, and surrender them to His safekeeping. Ask the Lord to infuse you with faith and the grace to trust His plan and purpose for you.

Even Jesus experienced fear in the garden, but He ultimately came to say, ". . . Not My will, but Yours be done." (Luke 22:42 NIV) It's not always an easy thing to lay down your fears, but God understands. He has only your best interests in mind and doesn't want to see you swallowed up in fear. Ask Him to give you more faith to meet the challenges of the day.

Faith is being certain of what you do not see. Faith releases us from fear; they cannot coexist. It's a confident assurance in God and His promises. Embrace faith while you do your best to give no place to fear. Let His perfect love cast out all your fears.

ROBIN DIX

Father God, you know the things in my heart and life that cause me to fear, and I'm so thankful that You understand. Please cause my faith to increase and my fears to decrease. Thank You for Your kindness and understanding regarding my weaknesses. Take me by the hand and show me the way. Amen.

28: BALM OF THE PSALMS

"Even when I walk through the darkest valley, I will not be afraid, for you are close beside me. Your rod and your staff protect and comfort me." (Psalm 23:4)

A balm is something that is used to soothe and comfort. The psalms do that as David and other writers become authentic and real in their cries to the Lord. Their worship and awe of God also comfort and soothe our souls.

Whenever you are troubled by the events in your life, the direction your life is taking, the endlessness of your symptoms, or the loss of friendships, turn to the book of Psalms. You will find yourself ministered to in their Holy-Spirit-inspired words.

The psalms can give you hope when things seem hopeless. They can encourage and lift you up in your times of pain and grief. They are a great reminder of how God knows us deeply and understands our suffering. He is not threatened by our tears or crying out to Him, even in anger.

The psalms are a gift of honesty in the brokenness of our world. When we call on Him in our times of trouble, He *will* rescue us! Sandra McCracken has a very soothing album called *Psalms* that I recommend. I also recommend using a highlighter as you go through the book of Psalms to mark verses that really speak to your heart.

Father God, I want to thank you for the comfort and healing that is found in the Psalms. When I am struggling with my illness I can always find Your heart of encouragement there. Speak to me through Your living Word. I praise you! Amen.

29: BREATH PRAYERS

"Never stop praying. Be thankful in all circumstances, for this is God's will for you who belong to Christ Jesus." (1 Thessalonians 5:17-18 NLT)

Breath prayers have been practiced for hundreds of years. It's a perfect way to pray without ceasing. It involves picking a word or phrase from scripture and praying it in conjunction with your breath. For example: focus on your breathing, **slowly** in and out. On the inhalation, say, "Lord." On the exhalation, say, "Have Mercy." This is just one example.

Here are some breath prayers you can use (taken from various sources):

Speak Lord, for Your servant is listening.

My help comes from the Lord, maker of heaven and earth.

Here I am, Lord.

Show Your power.

When I am afraid, I will trust you.

Not my will, but Yours.

Bring Your kingdom.

Say the word.

Come, Lord Jesus.

The Lord is my Shepherd; I shall not want.

Father, into Your hands, I commit my spirit.

In Christ alone, my soul finds rest.

Jesus, be the center.

Abba, I belong to You.

Creator, touch me with Your joy.

Holy God, help me live for You.

Gracious God, give me strength.

Holy Spirit, lead and guide me.

Show me Your way, O Lord.

These are just some examples. Take any short scripture and just divide it into two parts—one you say as you slowly inhale and the other as you slowly exhale. After a while, you will find yourself doing it without conscious thought.

Father God, thank You for Your Word, which is living and powerful and able to change my heart and mind. Help me to pray without ceasing, trusting You to change my heart, and help me experience Your love in a greater way than I ever thought possible. Amen.

30: COMPASSION AND EMPATHY

"But you, O Lord, are a God of compassion and mercy, slow to get angry and filled with unfailing love and faithfulness." (Psalm 86:15 NLT)

I love that God is a God of compassion, don't you? Empathy is the capacity to feel what others are feeling, and to understand what they're thinking. We are called as believers to not only rejoice with those who rejoice, but also to mourn with those who mourn. Empathy makes that possible. Compassion, on the other hand, is the ability to enter in with someone in their suffering.

Because God understands, feels compassion toward you, and gives you the ability to empathize with others, you should pray for opportunities to use them to minister to your fellow brothers and sisters who are also suffering with chronic illness. At the same time, you can ask God to bring people into your day, your life, to show empathy and demonstrate compassion towards *you*.

It's not enough to put yourself in someone else's shoes; you need to act on it. The comfort that God has shown you, you should use to comfort others. We are called to love others and show genuine compassion. Pity, quite often, involves elevating oneself above the one who is suffering, and can be condescending in attitude. Compassion enters in with the one who is suffering.

You are not called to do this in your own strength. If you tried, you would burn out rather quickly. Ask God to show empathy and compassion *through* you. Allow the Spirit to guide you as He brings people and needs to your mind.

ROBIN DIX

Father God, thank You for giving me the gifts of empathy and compassion. Bring the people into my life that You wish to minister to through me. Also, please bring people into my life that You have equipped to minister to me. I love You so very much! Amen.

31: YOUR LIFE IS A TAPESTRY

**"So we don't look at the troubles we can see now; rather, we fix our gaze on things that cannot be seen. For the things we see now will soon be gone, but the things we cannot see will last forever."
(2 Corinthians 4:18)**

Our life is like a tapestry. We only see the messy underside while God sees the beauty of the completed tapestry. He's creating something beautiful of your life, even in the midst of your illness. Even though life's a bit messy right now, the tapestry that is your whole life is becoming breathtakingly beautiful.

Every aspect of your life is necessary and being perfected moment by moment by the hands of a loving God. Corrie Ten Boom, author of *The Hiding Place*, was affiliated with this poem describing this very thing:

Life is But a Weaving

Corrie Ten Boom (The Tapestry Poem)

> *My life is but a weaving*
> *Between my God and me.*
> *I cannot choose the colors*
> *He weaveth steadily.*
> *Oft' times He weaveth sorrow;*
> *And I in foolish pride*
> *Forget He sees the upper*

And I the underside.
Not 'til the loom is silent
And the shuttles cease to fly
Will God unroll the canvas
And reveal the reason why.
The dark threads are as needful
In the weaver's skillful hand
As the threads of gold and silver
In the pattern He has planned.
He knows, He loves, He cares;
Nothing this truth can dim.
He gives the very best to those
Who leave the choice to Him.

Your life is a series of ups and downs, joys and sorrows, pain and pleasure. Even though you don't understand all that God is creating through your illness, take comfort in the fact that He doesn't waste anything you go through in your life.

Father God, be glorified in my life, every part of it. Help me to grow in my ability to trust you with all the details, both big and small. Thank You for weaving a beautiful tapestry with my life. Amen.

RESOURCES

Rest Ministries

In Spite of My Illness

The Mighty

Focus on The Family

Chronic Illness Bloggers

Guideposts Breath Prayers

Breath Prayers from the Bible

The Breath Prayer as a Means of Grace

Through the Fog

Write, Launch, and Market Your Book in 90 Days

Thank you for downloading my book! I really appreciate your feedback, and I look forward to hearing what you have to say.

URGENT PLEA! Please leave me an honest REVIEW on Amazon

Thanks so very much!

Robin
♥

ABOUT THE AUTHOR

Robin Dix has always enjoyed the written word and is very blessed to have had the opportunity to write this book. She lives with her husband and crazy cat in New Hampshire.

You can contact her at robindixwrites@gmail.com

SELF-PUBLISHING SCHOOL

NOW IT'S YOUR TURN

Discover the EXACT 3-step blueprint you need to become

a bestselling author in 3 months.

Self-Publishing School helped me, and now I want them to help you with this FREE WEBINAR!

Even if you're busy, bad at writing, or don't know where to start, you CAN write a bestseller and build your best life.

With tools and experience across a variety niches and professions, Self-Publishing School is the only resource you need to take your book to the finish line!

DON'T WAIT

Watch this FREE WEBINAR now, and Say "YES" to becoming a bestseller:

https://xe172.isrefer.com/go/sps4fta-vts/bookbrosinc3359

Made in the USA
Lexington, KY
16 November 2017